Arthur and Guinevere

Keith Harris

Published by Pending Press Ltd.

Arthur and Guinevere
copyright © Keith Harris 2013

All rights reserved.
No part of this book may be reproduced in any form without the permission in writing from both the copyright owner and the publisher.

Cover illustrations © Kate Cadman

This book is published by Pending Press Ltd.

ISBN 978-1-903466-06-3

Preface

It is with reluctance that I write a preface to this work. Some introduction is needed though because otherwise the themes are likely to be misunderstood. This is not romantic, epic or lyrical poetry. The verse can only be classified as mystical – poetry of the Night not of the Day.

Are the figures of Arthur and Guinevere allegorical? Is Arthur the male and Guinevere the female side of our own human natures? Perhaps. But I hope they may be conceived symbolically with more than one interpretation. Could Arthur be the physical and Guinevere the ethereal? Could Arthur be the spirit and Guinevere the soul? We can say that Arthur is king and Guinevere queen of the realm of Albion ... but this only begs the question of how 'Albion' is to be interpreted?

We can definitely say that the poems are Arthurian in the sense that Celtic Britain and the stories of the Round Table and the Grail quest set the scene. I have decided not to put in references. Those familiar with the Arthurian and Grail legends, with the Bible, William Blake and the Christian esoteric tradition springing especially from Rudolf Steiner and Valentin Tomberg can easily detect wider contexts.

Though I will mention here Arthur's sword, Excalibur. To calibrate is to measure, to be "ex-calibratable" is thus to be immeasurable and so Excalibur can be considered limitless. Arthur draws a sword from stone and in doing this he is recognised as the true king. This sword breaks. It is replaced by the sword from the Lake. The swords of stone and water. The swords of the knights defend the realm from evil and aggression just as the white blood cells defend the body from external encroachment and disease. While the red cells offer maternal sustenance to the rest of the organism. Symbolically speaking we might argue that 'the white wine' defends and 'the red wine' sustains the well being of the organism.

Near the borders of day and night the forces of the blood flow into human sexuality. The Freudian analyst is intent on uncovering the phallic element. But did not Jung, a psychoanalyst with a hungering for the mystical, say that the phallus itself is a symbol? An image perhaps also for forces active within the (k)nightly* defenders of the immunity system. Yet the blood can only care for the human organism when the white and the red forces are in balance, that is, when male and female processes in our organism work harmoniously together.

At the opening of the Third Millennium we are beginning to realise that we can only truly be human if the male and female sides of our nature are in balance. Just as we recognise that the forces of the child within us are needed if our adult selves are not to ossify. We might even express it thus, the forces of the night need to fructify those of the day.

This harmony between the male and the female on the one hand and between childhood and ageing on the other does not come about of itself. Are not great though hidden deeds even now being done at the boundaries where the Day and the Night encounter each other? And is it not possible that these encounters could become the stuff of poetry?

Throughout these poems there is a play on the words 'night' and 'knight'. Sometimes I have not even been sure myself which spelling to use.

---

* *nightly* – because these organic processes occur in the 'night', i.e. in the depths of unconsciousness. And *knightly* – because the immune system acts in ways compatible to the knights of the Round Table who fight against external aggression.

O Mensch, gib acht,
Was spricht die tiefe Mitternacht –
Ich sclief, ich schlief – aus tiefem Traum bin ich erwacht,
Die Welt ist tief, noch tiefer als der Tag gedacht,
Tief ist ihr Weh,
Die Lust – noch tiefer als das Herzeleid –
Weh spricht – Vergeh,
Doch alle Lust will Ewigkeit, will tiefe, tiefe Ewigkeit.
  (Friedrich Nietzsche: Nachtlied)

O Man, take heed,
What says the Night:
"I slept, I slept – from deep dream am I awoken";
The world is deep, deeper than the Day conceives,
Deep is her woe;
Yearning – deeper yet than woe –
Woe says, "Depart,"
But every yearning wants eternity, profound eternity.
  (Nietzsche: Song of the Night)

To the Maid of the Mystic Now

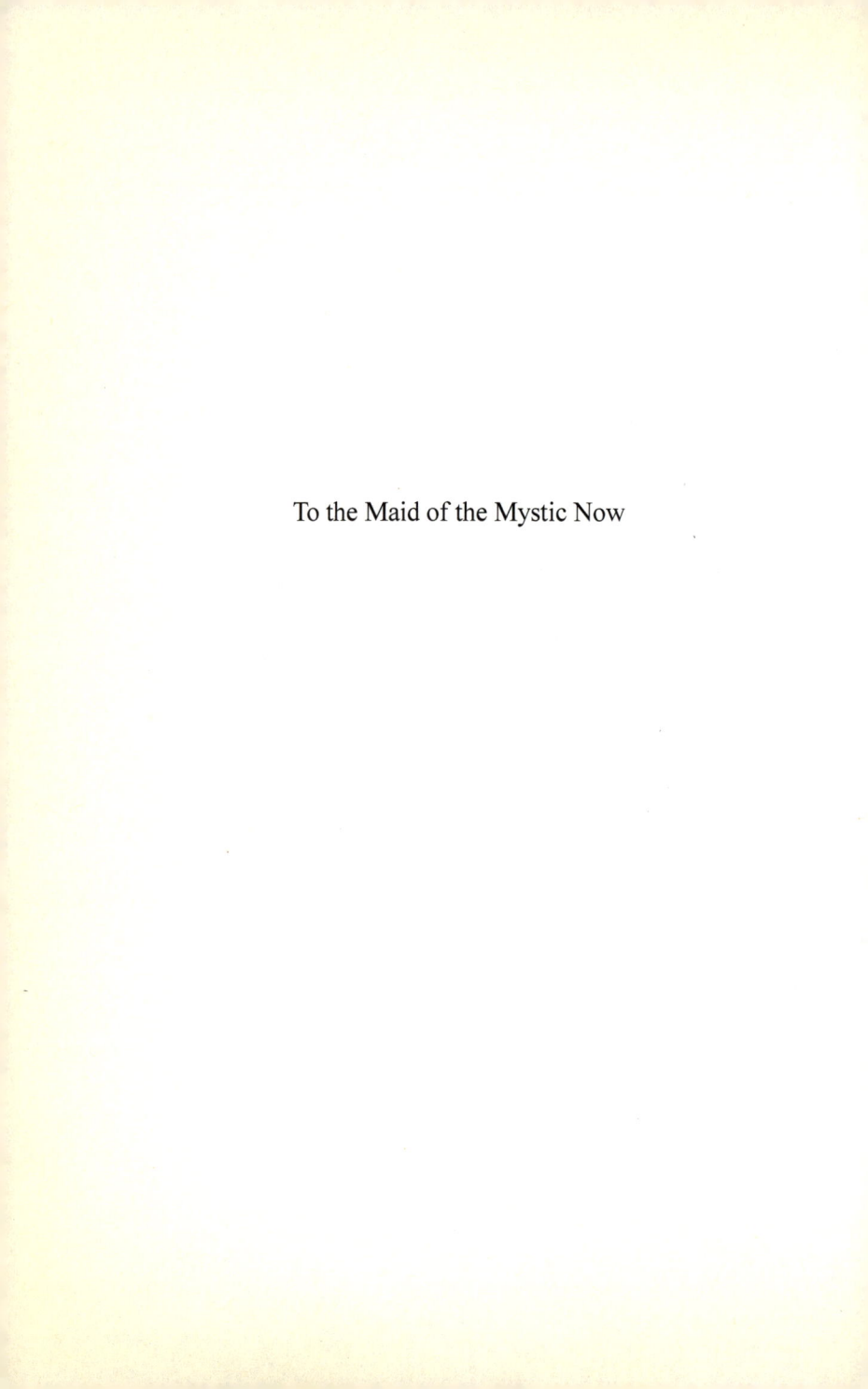

Arthur
Part I

1.

Rigid as a jut of rock
on Tintagel's granite fast
gazing at spray from wave
breaking over wave, bulge and surge
ebb and swell, swell and ebb,
sombre in solitude
hunched beside the ocean's ceaseless
groan ... till twilight dissolves in dark.

2.

While my knights fend off furies
in ancient forest vast
I, yoked to kingship
of this realm, frailly lean
upon my human sediment.

3.

Troubled deeper than sorrow
by this orb, this pulse
of silence present
above the cross of my
unsheathed and glistening sword.

4.

Only the elements (winds
echoing in the womb of waves
surf swirling over granite outcrop
surges gurgling in stone clefts)
only the elements (infusing
forms of faery-fire
along lonely Celtic shores)
only the elements (wavering
invisibly behind
waving boughs and leafy rustle)
only the elements
sigh
rages of sleepy gratitude
for my sceptre's secret solace
which whispers promises
to where winds wane
within cold chasm-deeps
and where breathe fades
in human fibre's
gradual asphyxiation
to die in the hidden marrow
as blood is ever born
anew in living hollows
of human bone.

5.

Westward magenta woos
the ocean's wide receptacle
for our sky's rotund and dying
sun – red portal
to a second ethereal sea.

6.

From my tower beneath the steady
homeward flight of fowls
above gardens, green shady groves
and woods settling with twilight's wonder,
within these walls man-built
of man-hewn stone
I begin my solitary watch.

Before me nature's broad way
is breached by luscious flood
but I am not of nature.
Ever before me sways
temptation
snap this sceptred unity
and die
or sleep with nature.

7.

Slumber beckons me
toward lavish unrestrained
non-being.
Flow out my breath
and warmth of blood
let Arthur's skeleton
be desiccated as dust,
let Arthur's marrow
crave only cold stone.
And yet Sir Gawain and Sir Bors
each of my Table's knights
alone, weary, battle-stiff
staggering from pre-feudal forest
tears trickling against the gales
till each faints and falls
into a fallow sleep
forgetting and forgiving all.
How their jousts would waste
quashed beneath the passing chase
mired under muddied stumbles
glutted by low glory-hunts,
knightly victories or conquests
quick and cowardly,
wounds or defeats all seeping
away in unsung history,
each embarked quest would sink
untraceably beneath
time's thankless passing
into the mere
of the gone as

with their loss of now
adventures die.

Our knights battles would puff
nothingwards
but for this moment chaliced
in Excalibur's limitless
offering.

8.
Behind my back Camelot's burghers
toss barely disguised snides
"Arthur is discouraged."
"Aye, lacking courage."
"Arthur is aged."
"Ha! An impotent king, see
even his wife prefers his courtiers'
embraces to his."
"His weapon is never battle-wet."
"It sags nodding at the soil."

Not so, my friends, and yet
I must not speak for I
hold tongues burning beneath
consciousness, I am bound.
My wife, 'tis said, lies
with my knights and not with me.

My subjects wag
with whispers of my cowardice
but I must not speak,
I must not issue forth to
broach too subtle truths
casting pearls (won
from tear-filled watches)
before burly burghers who
in Camelot's boisterous market
prattle among their snorting swine.
Nor must I slink away
retreating from those malice-soaked asides
spoken to be overheard.
I must remain in the very upright
centre of my royal calling
at that post between heaven's high
participation in sense-denuded night
and her daily disappearance
with dawn.

I must not speak, I must not
move, manoeuvre or remove
though rumours abound about my
non-emergence in the joust.
"Excalibur is not battle-scarred."
True my friends but listen,
those who may, to silent speech:
Excalibur is never wielded
because Excalibur wields.
No passive sword, cold

metal carried into combat
acted on by active hands,
no passive sword but sceptre
(unseen by self-seeking eyes
and ego-flated selves)
my blade is the flaming upright
its forging never finished
for in its wielding stillness
a presence knights our quests –
togetherness present this night
outside day's raw relief
inside the unheard passing
of each human time.

                          9.*

We fight and sleep – only Arthur
awake in the starlit dark
rounds goodly combat to outer
reaches of the realm.
Our strivings require no proclamation,
deeds of lost knights need no squire
to brag their bravery abroad
for in Excalibur's refulgence
once burning quests and questions
of night's hungering heart
are steadfast in the passionate
presence of the now.

10.
Traversing the land
wave in wave, breeze
through breezes, wind within
the four winds, storm in
tempest, ebb in flows and flow
in time's of ebbing – mysteriously
tracing nature's nocturnal need
a higher hereness resonates
with the thunder of the sword
alive in stone.

11.
Hung with the weight of my gilded
iron crown, my head nods
with oncoming waves of swooning –
yet even now I remember
my nearest and dearest, my Guinevere,
loves Lancelot.

Gaunt cheeks and tears' salt
alone speak of grieving
for my dream-steeped queen.
I see but call no cue
of seeing. Who sees
Arthur's sorrow bearing anon
upon the crowned bearer of the sword
drawn twice from stone?

12.

By and by and ever
before me sways
this vale's sleepy lull.
Temptation partially withdrawn
and endlessly drawn out,
sweetening not to be
for nature
but not for me.

Yet to lie
dreaming as Gawain and Bors
of a virgin's ache
in virgin womb.

13.

In these lonely watches even heaven
sometimes seems to dream
or to be
a dream
a dream dreaming me
through dreams,
an image of an image reflected
in densities of death.

14.
The ease to grip and rip apart
the needle's eye of unity
and slide
down
downwards
lower, lower through wells
welling lush and loose
with nature and unlaborious
scents sweaty
with conjugality.

15.
Guinevere, my missing queen,
how oft have I wished to wake
and take you to me
and tell of my night's solitude
where my knight's pains become
my pain and of how their dying
quests are sacrificed
in this Immeasurable pyre.

16.
My Lady white and true to night
Arthur so long has longed
for a heavenly touch of you.

17.
In midnight desolation
I hardly more discern
if this is death with life
or life in death.

18.
Amfortas
Was it a dream or did I hear
my own voice calling
the name of Amfortas
at the very brink of slumber?

My brother, thou sore, speared
and unpitied Fisher King,
in blind obscure night I am
awake, my blood bleeds
through the fourfold chalice
of a faint and fluctuating heart,
its flow not dammed, its rhythmic
whisper not impure,
no urges erupt as abscess
in too-finished flesh.

Amfortas, your agony cries out
to me from the not-yet-come
and begs me even this day's dark

to learn why, why my struggle
(as a stream of sorrow sojourning
my pulse's never-ending beat)
does not trespass
to morass
my aching corporeal uncertainty
with wound like yours
impossible to staunch
and ever festering.

Your bloody portrait pairs
my nightly hours with pain;
descending 'neath hearkened dark
our hurt – yours lacerate
of body, mine of soul –
sobs forth this knowledge
uncitable for sight:
My sufferings hold within my heart
only because Guinevere lies
with my nights and not with me.

Else I though king
would be unable,
else my straining station
as the very hammer of Tubul Cain
would pound in her sweet whines
and die me
to unfastness,
else would I

(devoid of Excalibur's
infallibility)
abdicate
and plunge
this seething brand
into desire's black burning
and smog would foul the
precious vale of Avalon
with countless particles
of soot.

And gushing laughter of my queen
would herd us both
in ever stagnating circles
pawning selves in unchaste chase
where two (and neither a one)
are kneaded to a
mere oozing us,
would condemn us both to beg
for death in sleep.

Amfortas, my queen is not Kundry.

Though Galahad is unborn and the Grail
the future's embryo,
we also may dream of then
when you and I
when two – a king and queen,

and each a royal, that is,
a human self – can wait
(as Parsifal and Condwiramours)
through three still wakening nights
starry, ethereal, warmth:
Two together one
yet each a uniquely living
independent self.

Upon beatific thresholds
is hallowed
a heavenly third.

Lohengrin …

Three tears of nearness
unify
what we were
with who
our hearts will bear.

Amfortas, my queen is not Kundry.

19.
Guinevere, my only romance,
I will not upbraid
if your unbraided hair
rubs
perspirations of my nights.
Sleep sweetly with my thoroughbreds,
only by day give my
glancing I
such glances of your eye
to keep me unenthralled
by other women's charms,
give me dew-touches of your morning's
melody to hold back the white
wine's cunning effulgence
when, if riled by female smile,
my imaginary whiles
flirt concupiscently
with other women's wiles.

20.
May my imaginary whiles
recall you, Lady
pristine white and sighing
for sacramental night.

21.
I will wash each morn
that no tear stains my ageing face
as through this cross tormenting
day with night all remnants
of lukecool resent vaporise
within the scabbard of my sword.
Each morn I will rise
and work to love you anew
and my words, double-edged
as my blade, will never jab
myself in you.

22.
Behind closed curtains come
crude jibe and jest:
"Arthur is old."
"Too old to fight in frays."
"Too old to make fay
with his fair queen!"
"He is not bold."
"Not bold enough to stand!"

They do not know of silent
sleeplessness when all eyes
close and selves breathe
with their beloved's breath,
I watch alone.

23.
Our prayers incandescent
around the Measureless Sword
centre compassion and become
the High Table
of my knights' each lonely quest.

24.
Here in Camelot I am crowned
my subjects heed my every command.
"Whose castle is this?"
"Arthur's," comes the answer.
No one, it seems, knows
that I, who am king, own nothing.
In nightly vigil where are rich
tapestries and treasuries of the day
gone by?

Even the silken-clad queen
sleeping at my side dreams
herself in Lancelot's strong arms
dates his potent embrace.

Nothing is mine save
wakefulness. I
have left all to stand
struck in stony poverty.

Excalibur alone I hold
and this but held in trust.
(For who may grasp the immeasurable?)
My sword is not my own, only
leant for knightly hours
of remembrance.

25.
Whence comes Excalibur?
"From the waters," says one.
"From the stone," says a second.
"No that luckless, rock-sheathed blade
rusted and broke in battle," says a third.
They do not know, Arthur
is not fickle
but one sword was his,
is his.
The sword I drew effortlessly forth
from spell-bound stone
glowing as celestial vision pierced
circles of Albion's well-guarded,
jewelled crown and my young self received
kingship of the realm and guardianship
of nature's rugged shore and her valley's
faery forest ways, that sword
drawn from its tomb of stone
became brittle in few days
to break upon a battlefield.

(Only fools do not know
the sword will break
which no love sows.)

Borne to me by our Lady
of the rippling Lake
this sword (whose measurements
the starry heavens make)
is not another
but the blade-in-stone reforged,
reborn from that weapon fragmented
by the flight of time.
The same unspoken name
is etched in glowing golden runes
upon its rust-freed resilience.

By day this speech is silent
its gilded lettering fades
in silvery formlessness.
Only by night
along lonely barriers of wave and rock
by water and by stone
within the sacred crystallising
of fiery breath
does Excalibur's gledeing
malleability become
the keeper of our knightly quests.

(Only a fool does not know
the sword will break
where no love glows.)

                26.

I can never conceive
how time sans sequence and heavy
with waves implacable,
how time in night's sleepless hours
can elapse
that grey once more lightens
into deepest, deepest blue
and birds begin to sing.

                27.

Between lithe swaying steps
my wife's smile hides
presentiment. Forgotten prophecies
amuse her mutely worded song,
her singing pregnant
with presentiments
not present
for my day's continual loss
of time.

28.

I know existence only
through the skull.
My body stiff moves without joy.
How may I with meaning hold
my morning or my evening queen?

Yet I almost believe a ray
from the Immeasurable has smote
my wakefulness with sleep
or how could I walk
each day among my courtiers,
my subjects who have slept with
Proserpina's linger
fresh upon unfurrowed youthful
brows, my friends who look to me
as rightful king, their gaunt
and swiftly ageing Sire.

29.

In Camelot's sedate gravity day's chores,
day's feasts, day's music move
relating human hours
to the sun's steady curve across her sky.
Harpers strum minor chords and chant
lays of ancient chivalry. And as our minds
accompany their song, partings
of sweet romance or calls to chilling
combat come alive
within our inner day:
Tabernacles spun for knighthood's
courtly joys are present
on imagined fighting fields

*... fields which to our outer senses
are clogged with fleshless
bones beneath the turf,
bones in furloughs of forgotten ruts,
bones of dismembered forefathers
today but lime for soil.*

---

* We can envisage the poems in italics as being spoken by the chorus of the knights of the Round Table.

Arthur
Part II

1.

None of my Table's knights gather
now to tell their news.
Rarely are their names recalled
yet all know
our adventures, our victories, all
we did but prepared this time of crisis
where every Sir by self alone
this day
seeks for the Grail.
The Grail – beckoning and fostering
aspirations yet to be fulfilled.

2.

Even my wife, under darkened archways
of our ancient stone-cold crypt
before the altar seven candlelit,
even my still youth-fair queen kneels
begging Heaven's Queen for mysterious
intercessions
of the Sangreal.

3.

None but I and the maid she
fondly grumbles about:
"And always complaining!"
"What does she say, my dear?"
"Nothing!"
"Er, nothing?"
"But the way she says nothing
makes me start complaining
about myself.
And her lineage! The
shepherd's cast-off
that's for sure!"

I'm glad the shepherd maid is here,
listening to my wife happily
bitch about her brings
me my only daytime smiles.

And last night as I strove in darkness
to hold my sword raised
just when my hands could no longer
stay steady and Guinevere tossing,
sighing and sliding her warm
thigh over mine –
I pursed my lips and muttered,
"King Arthur's queen but a fawning
receptacle for the sowing
of Lancelot's wild oats."

Suddenly that maid's eyes
vivid as stars in blackest night
were upon me … and I guess
I remembered my task.

                4.

None but I and the maid
Guinevere vehemently dotes on
know of my queen's silent sessions of prayer
deep in the dimness of the crypt.
And I cannot but deem her earnest whispers
yearn for chivalry's lost dawn
and not just for a quick return
of knight escorts and the gay flirtations
that once reigned about her
for when I look and listen in these
dreary vaulted arches as she kneels
before the altar's seven candles
round the rough-hewn Celtic cross
her posture's trembling poignancy
resembles more a mother's care
than woman's languor
all allure for knightly bedding
... and of course those afternoon rides
in the wood with Lancelot.
But wait! That maid, the one Guinevere delights
to groan about, has a way of looking
across you without quite
looking at you.

5.
Arthur's Lament
Under silken cover sullenly I lie
staring at ruins near sleep's dull verge
my wife moaning winsome at my side
dreaming herself in plays of seek and hide
laughing and pouting through romance's surge
as she dons courtly dues of caress and sigh:
dallying in rose gardens with my young knights
till slides of amour drown those sunset sights.

6.
Through our bedchamber
barren as the taper's ash
breath gestures moist
clouds of numbness
over these our
half-neglected nights.

7.
Our fraternity ventures, each for himself,
through wilderness and plagued infertile soil.
Though disappeared from daytime senses
a secret sacredness renews
each Sir's presence at his seat.
Wooden no longer but alive unseen
our Table's cambium retreat

breathes round breadths of Albion
inspiring each knight's courage for his quest
expiring with every cut and blow
as within the breastplate and the helm
a human self wakens
to human want.

8.

Though gloom glowers
through marsh and morbid tracts, gloats
round heaving negligence,
luminous edges nightly borne
rain rainbow hues of shining life
as knights in righteous quest
hew mettled conscience
through fields of crawling things.

Though murk maims
remorselessly, mauls
unremittingly,
fragrance is freed and colours
quiver as knightly threshold heralds
the unperceived drama of love
forever absolving
death.

9.

Nourished by adventure
quests, whose meaning is invisible
as light, return nocturnally
to the Shrine of Chivalry –
so secretly being
born
within Avalon's misty welling
forth of times yet to be.

10.

From flights where slight misjudgements
frieze in death,
each choice of conscience shrives
pain's bounty to a twine of light.
In combat of good 'gainst bad
through scenes of vital ever-active form
colours come to genesis,
every static stroke or defect darkens,
and every dowdy streak within the shimmering
registers a miss of mercy
where some cowardly cringe
or glory lust (or perhaps
some other kind of lust)
swayed in to hold opaque
flickers of holy inwardness.

11.
Those other hazes, lounging
half aware and clinging greedily
to their renown,
dull staining lulls – distemper
in our living stream.
Our knightly current where in
clear wakened dream by deeds
of waking conscience rendered selflessly
seeds are sown in the
holy soil of holy night
to pyre Albion's bloodied shrouds
to purest light.

12.
In undergrowths of fungal-morbid forest
the fittest struggling inhumanly
to survive as Klingsor's cripples
sever and join up, splicing
according to abstract plans spawned
by their skulls merely
to amass more coin.

For Klinsorian systems and minds
limited to strictures of the brain
nature is seen as neuter
not as she. So chemical constituents
are callously to be extracted.

Double-spirals ripped out and
ripped apart, riven from Natura's
faery-fostered alchemy.
Their goal: Manipulated grain
leprous as self-destructing lice.

Undergrowths of fungal-morbid
forest are to spread
throughout this and every other
fay-fair realm …
is this dream
or dream becoming day?

                         13.
Dull, darkened and diminished
fettered strains
Klingsor designed –
his grasping cripples lurch
their heavy girths across
the hidden way
to quash the flow of life
to pulp.

14.

Who hears through the ringing echoes
of sword on shield
as human hearts pound
above the gore?
Who listens to battle furies,
who heeds lonely tournament
where youth's first eager flush
with manhood's starker self
gives way to warts and wounds
and byways beckon passing lives
... pastimes in nameless undergrowth
mazes sullen with similarity
whose only decider is the I?
Who gathers unfinished quests
of our forgotten nights
as we endure to furthermost straits –
homeless knights suffering to staunch
torn peripheries of Albion?

15.
Contests wrought to protect
plundered vestiges of Albion await
Excalibur's stern chastisement.
Its razor fire cleaves
good from bad, leaves
boundary where verity
is gleaned and viciousness
vanquished, frees selves
from motives enslaved
by libidinous sloth and dreary
inconsequence.

Its fire raises
knighthood's nightly path –
every fearful, feckless, feeble lunge
or leer impaled on pseudo-stature,
unconscious chaff around
long-conscienced grain,
cindered
well before ways weave
that starry spiral womb
which announces
to Camelot
her child to be.

16.
Not old, cold metal in emboldened
hands, not Arthur
but his poverty in prayer
cradles
the immeasurable centre
 of the Table Round.

Seeds of day-quests resound
within the unseen space of sleep,
the needle's I rings
unpredictable phases of transition
as night's heavenly periphery
is reborn
within the point.

17.
Deep within our frays only
pity cups life unborn,
only mercy can tender presence,
can pass tenderly to be
present: Raised in sacrificial upright
nature is undone (the serpent held
within the spine)
the snake of time caught
above the rend of battle
by each human bearer
of the Mosaic Staff.

18.

Each knight harbours a portion
of the presence, a portion of
the promise – No! no portion
but the whole for unreservedly
the Sword Immeasurable radiates
within each true knight's star.

19.

Hidden in hollow depths of human form
Excalibur mettles human marrow:
the Midnight Sun ensouled
in unfilled space
as knightly threshold gledes
the dark with light.

20.

Battle wounds caught
in the brine of empathy arise
with alchemical patent …
rainbows retrace
recondite ways toward
Chivalry's unsited origin.

21.

While hearts pine
homecoming penance
morbidity flees
the proximity of the light
which sees.

22.

Rainbows sigh
for Heaven's silent arch.
Acts, whose numbers can never account,
obedient when chaliced
by Arthur chaste beside his queen –
a higher reign repeals
imbalances in mediocrity,
horizontal additions and subtractions
quantities clinically celebrate
disappear in the crucible
when a flower's tiny
pollinated seed becomes a shoot
of the mustard tree.

23.
*From the realms' far reaches
impoverished of all that's won or lost
our quests return
to Chivalry's recondite beginning.
Dark opened by unselfish sight,
colours shimmer
around the sacrament whose altar
is invisible light.*

24.
*As sword steel clashes
heights ring in depths,
Excalibur, echoing the
immeasurable moment
of the Midnight Hour
carries our future into now.*

25.
Hours of patient compassion bless
knight-combat's lightning response.
As time is moved
by non-reciprocated eternity
the coming blow is known
before it strikes.

26.

Who is worthy, who
not fearful
to stand or fall prostrate
beneath the firmament, that dome
fermenting knightly quest
through white incendiary heat
to tensile steel?
None has the worth, none
the weight to await
that weightless pyre
but shackled with cares and burdens of
the daytime realm Arthur is crowned and must
rein in returning wounds
... when thresholds are lost
to night and our hours'
quotidian lukecool
crawl begins.

27.

Arthur steadfast in the day
of conscious night – lesions
of office liaise
to the core of time –
he trembles
before that boundary which bears
the utterness
of now.

28.
*Our only staff of nighthood
the Sword Immeasurable testifies
to the miracle of man,
of man who walks in nature
drinks her waters, tastes her fruits
but he is not of nature
for in Excalibur's flame
nature is undone:
Human substance becomes
the miracle of earth
and unknown night alights
within today.*

29.
*Excalibur
our only staff of knighthood
drenched with a linger of
the human form divine.*

30.
Where is our Sword's crowned guardian?
Arthur watches
dead to night in day he knows
the miracle of man –
of bravery, of wounds, of lances
of all we through our combat-quests endure
to defend our dying world
as one by one we trudge
lonely toward
my-time-to-die.

31.
Beside him lies his sleeping queen
does she help? Whose wisdom
is wise enough to know?
But Arthur knows
his office doomed, our quests
to perish all unless,
unless another steadies the ague
of his ageing grip.

32.

*Arthur holds
the Miracle of Man.
With tears so helpless
in an old man's I
his poverty perceives
this single hope:
the Miracle of Woman.*

Guinevere

1.

Last night I saw
or is it every night I see
my king's isolated vigil
as against lack of firmness he strives
to hold his unsheathed sword
upright.

Ageing in taciturn loneliness
he knows me
not.
He thinks I am too fatigued
with courtly ways of courting on his knights
to court with him,
too preoccupied with fantasies of
Lancelot to feel his need
of piercing concern, his tiring
manhood's rage.

How deaf he is
to my laughter peeling
in our chamber as I lie
with him, above him, undoing
the wilful stiffness of his day.

2.

As his resolve begins to ebb
as his resilience loses
tensile mettle,
as he glances at my sleeping form
and a pearly tear glistens
in his I
then my laughter smiles
I too am peace-filled beside him,
as his hands hilted
with impatience tremble
mine I place with his
and take his sword's beaten warmth
into myself – quiet, quiet
beyond our motion's tenderest tremor
I am with him more awake
than he (though in his dotage
he believes I snore).

3.

I entwine
to open with inwardness
the martial line of fire
with Guinevere's help
Excalibur lances to a chalice
begging heavenwards.

4.

How long have we sought together
Arthur and Guinevere –
long, long before we knew
our search rested
on but one hope …

How foolish his complaint that I flaunt
my queenly offices around
with his young officers and use up
my days only (as he falsely construes)
to languish in sleep's soft sighs
while he so mustily
insomnias his nights.

Dotage, my Lord!
Your sight sees day's senile sense
mine
night's ever youthful star.

5.

And his petty jealousies of Lancelot,
does he not realise Guinevere
is childless and children
come from somewhere?
My affections for my Lancelot
bear my love for our children
those babes we never yet have held.

6.

Rachel weeps
for her children
because she so long
like Guinevere
was childless.

7.

By day I imagine my Lancelot (and how often
have you not, my ageing husband,
called him your son!)
I picture him far, far from our home
riding into battle for adventure.
By dreaming dark I see him anew
his son, with wings upon his shoulders,
hovers near. This son promises
his appearance to me
in faith then I follow
falling into deepest slumber
releasing the Guinevere
in Guinevere
to night's maidenly vigil –
lonely too for from Arthur's side
comes not a sigh of thanks.

Though from elsewhere I sense
sacred echoes lightening
our task as Arthur's angel runes
with Guinevere this arch planted
in the star-filled firmament.

8.

All night we labour
and just ere morn recalls
her Guinevere
I kiss Arthur's tears
drying on his sweat and
thank him for his help.

Too quickly, it seems, my daytime
puts my night to sleep,
my soul drifts lightly
with the billowing cloud
and hums with songs of birds.

While from our bed Arthur drags
that stiffness in his legs
(and that sop between them)
to his dim sense of day
– hiding in courtly silence
bitter reproaches against his wife.

9.

As day further undresses
my night, I engage in courtly
manners, performing all courtly
service for the Order of our knights
with courtships (seen and unseen)
spelling rounds of courtly amour.
My flirtations rousing
one to red-blooded emotional
flagellation, while leaving
suicidally sad
another of our knights.

10.

Sometimes stricken
by the shallowness of courtly conceits
my longing to conceive surfaces
and I stray upon lonely ways
toward the lapping waters and otherworldly
linger of our Welsh lakeside.

Was this the Lake from which
the Lady brought forth Excalibur
– or was that tale but
fairytale made up by Merlin before
dotage took him, dotage for
that fay-fair, sunshine-singing maid
(who could have been, and who knows
maybe was, his great-great granddaughter).
She left him worn out, senile
sans sense and voiceless
trapped within the mighty oak.
A most fitting cell, I deem,
for lecherous old men.

11.

Winds and mist grey hills surround
this lonely Celtic mere.
I have commanded my maid to wait
upon my waiting from afar – yet
why do I wait beside this water?
And who is that maid
I took into my service? And when was it –
recently or long ago?

My memories toss me hither, thither,
whither I know not where ... I am
unable to recall if they
like lake-waves come fresh as the moment
or endure ancient as the sea
swirling over granite rock.

She was colourless, quiet,
lowly birth for sure
and somehow I can never be certain
why with my word, I
affirmed her stay.

12.

As afternoon draws on and Autumn
crests of colour weave
into the light over this lake, and
yet another night with Arthur looms
drawing up its drawbridge
like a key locking
a chastity belt –
as we once more strive to hold
upright to the star-signed heavens
this sacred vessel (still
believed by him
to be an iron sword).

Such labour and he so tacit
and thankless! Oh, painful
painless bed with a husband
without a tongue
who opens his mouth only to
gawk and not to kiss
our nocturnal nearness
with dialogues
of tender nestling.

13.

My tears salty as the sea
slip into the ripples washing
my cold and icy, naked feet –
why Arthur do you leave
Guinevere to herself
as I, childless, surround myself
with sporting attentions of young
Gallants. Wait! Is that
the shepherd maid coming to her
Lady Guinevere with some sore news
some message from I know not where
to wake fresh woes. But
can she still be so youthfully
maiden after all these years or
when was it now
she came to serve?

14.

Is she smiling? I feel her
smile as the lightness of a lay
never yet blessed by human voice
or a song recalled from youth's
limitless effervescence –
or that melody upon my lips this morn
which teased fresh saline flows
of childhood's joys or sorrows
and left me in wonder – wondering if
just as Arthur is blind
to the sight of sleep's awesome
otherworld perhaps I too fail
to hearken to an angelic presence
above this sword transformed
into a chalice by the night.
Am I, Guinevere, deaf to harmonies
metamorphosing our vessel to a
sceptre for the realm
in midnight hours?

15.

She approaches, her movement
grace-filled as gestures of warm moist breath,
unhindered as a silvery fish darting
against the current,
certain as rain falling
to the earth. Her footfall
feathery yet firm, even so decisive
that I have seen her shoeless print
indented into rock
as if she'd pressed it
upon damp soil.

And her fleetness – Arthur has sworn
she drifted through the hall leaving
her glance upon him, even though I know
she was bending behind the hedge cupping
dew-filled roses in her hands.

16.
My mood quickens when she's near
thinking becomes vibrant and alive
poised, meek yet open
to unsuspected nuances
of transposition.
Sometimes I think I only think
when she is by my side.

But where is she? I must dry
my glistening lids before
she glimpses her weeping queen.
I will not play the drooping
adolescent under her gaze.

17.
How long have we unknowingly
and half-knowingly sought,
apart by day beside by night,
for our one aspiration – that this
chalice forged of hope
in shame and falling
heavenwards
be blessed by a single ray
of that which knightly song reveres
as the Sangreal ...
Yet only emptiness, it seems,
fills out our everyday.

18.

I wander through the Great Hall
sombre in these sorrow-drenched days
and deprived of flowery decoration,
the harper's harmonies no longer heard.
Each time entering I seek
to avoid the awkward sight of
Chivalry's rotund relic
today without a knight at any seat
yet never yet have passed without my heart
violing wild exultation
as unbidden my eye rests
upon that chair where all our hopes
are placed. Even while passing
swiftly by
I am prostrate
before the Siege Perilous.

19.

My husband too, how often
chancing unawares
have I met him in the Great Hall
sunken on his stool, his I
enthralled
his eyes mutely and so sadly
pondering
the Dangerous Chair –
and we embarrassed quickly
gone our separate ways.

Oh why, Arthur, is your love
for Guinevere just so much
hoarfrost? (Sometimes I think
it were better for us all
if he put his ass
upon the Perilous Seat.)

But no, I am called
to be queen. I will draw
with my ageing king beyond
night's bridge to newest day
– though emptiness seizes
every mourning for our sons
(and for my Lancelot).

20.

I will aspire to remember each child
pursuing the holy quest.
It will be according to heaven
I shall fill my nightly raiment
and dare to take my place beside
Albion's sober solitary king:

At that space in time where
Arthur weds his Guinevere
our marriage cup offers
to the firmament
the free untainted future
of maid conjoined with man
that every knightly wound and sore
may heal.

The Lady's Maid

1.
I am the Maid disguised
as lady's maid
to serve Arthur's queen for his knights'
sickly realm.

2.
It is I who release
Guinevere from dynastic gossip
and that courtly dalliance
dominating the melodramas of her day.

3.
Oh, queen for Arthur's nights
I am the saline tear in your smile
the dew within your shining eye
and resolve's undetected
touch
trembling in your sighs.

4.
I am Celtica
bereaved of the voice of bards,
widowed, mute and waiting
beside mountain, moor,
forlorn and solitary mere.

5.
The Druid spirit sacrificed
to wean the present
from the past
so the lightning strike
can thunder from what is
yet to be.

6.
I lead your straying steps
toward lonely lakeside dreams
with rippling waters
rivulets cold and clear
misty faded colours
of Welsh hill and dale
reawakening love
for Arthur's so neglected nights.

7.
I no longer inspire poetry or music
even my sobs for that suffering child,
my cries for man
resounding in the angelic empyrean
bring no pause to heady plans
of servile politicians
and their banker-lords.

8.
My voice is silence,
for each knight of the realm
(and each brawny burly burgher)
must be free to heed
or not to heed
night's missing memory.

9.
How many in their sleep
weep at my hem
only to wake and turn forthwith
from wonder to the world
of monotone and calculating motives?

10.
How many
in this tear-sodden vale
know
each and every human soul
is exiled
from her heavenly home?

11.
How many know
the night is in travail
to bring to birth
the day to be?

12.
I am midwife
for the mood of questioning.
Maid or man
how will you encounter
answers
if you have no question?

13.
I am midwife for
shining clouds invisible
to sense-seeing eyes.

14.
I am midwife
for the forgotten faery sight
lingering near wilder ways
at the dawn and dusk of days.

15.
I am midwife for
for lost Celtic light
and the ethic of ethereal retreats
unnoticed
by the sense-clenched I.

16.
I am midwife for
the magic altruism of adolescence,
for the freshness of the child
slumbering in maid and man.

17.
How can you live so parched
so stunted and shorn off
from the one
who you once were?
How can you exist
deprived
of idealism's bubbling springs?

18.
My tears fall upon the five
evergreen paths to wisdom's
ancient recondite pool.
My tears trickle
for human egos,
for adults barred from childhood's
holy sleep.

19.
I am midwife
for recognising
Easter's radiance.
Effulgence invisible
to the sense-drenched I.

The Easter radiance
as unclaspable
as love.

20.
Beside the loneliness of Celtic lochs
beside minstrels brooding with Celtic myth
I whisper with your song.
My voice, unheard, in chorus
with the beating heart
breathing overtones
from bardic nights
as nature's living pulse
permeates
daytime senses
and pain is pregnant
with the birth of selves.

21.
I am the breeze between
these lapses into ordinariness,
the Mere's surface moved
by wind to waves
my sigh of troubled yearning
weds
ethereal temperaments
to the drifting
away of worldly hours.

22.
Beside the hymnal solitude
of waters and of wind
I am Vivian
Lady of the Lake
bequeathing
spontaneity in selfless love.

23.
I am the Lady of the Lake
in my hands the Sword Immeasurable
is unsheathed,
in silence
deep as night in day
Excalibur arises
from the waters of life.

24.
The sharp and glistening mettle
departing Arthur's aged
battle-torn and dying limbs
is thrown high above the waves …
the two-edged blade is borne
into the water's bosom,
clasped by my hand
the Sword so measureless
is sheathed.

25.
I am the Maid
disguised as maid
serving Arthur's queen for
his nights' sake.

26.
It is I who release
the Guinevere in Guinevere
from courtly dalliance
and her dry mundane days.

27.
Oh, queen for Arthur's knights
I am the sunrise
smiling through your tears
and true love's secret touch
upon the threshold of the quest.

28.
I am your guide to truest union,
marriage – the mystery immutable
between maid and man her mate.

Two, in trust in time,
love
in eternity
as night's hallowed heights
open for the sob of
human hearts.

29.
I am Rachel
weeping for my children,
shedding saline dew
for earthly man.

I am Rachel
maid to the Virgin
of Israel
and sweet mourner
for the Now in time.

30.
I am sister to Isis
who, since the return of
Easter radiance
within
the gentle passing away of time,
may lift
this very eve
the veil which hides
the ever-burning flame
of Now.

31.
For I am the Lady's Maid
handmaid of Mary Sophia
the Mother whose Son
has suffered
and is suffering still
the cross
of Gethsemane's eternal bloody night.

I am maid to
Mater Dolorosa
Handmaiden of God.